WILD TURKEY

TAME TURKEY

WILD TURKEY
TAME TURKEY

By DOROTHY HINSHAW PATENT

Photographs by
WILLIAM MUÑOZ

CLARION BOOKS

NEW YORK

ACKNOWLEDGEMENTS

The author and photographer want to thank the following for their help with this project—Pat Miller, Charles Cheff, Darrell Thurnbeck, the Musters, Richard Vaughan, Geoff and Brooke Prinz, Bob Sevilla, Jim Cunningham, Lindskoog Hatchery, Nicholas Turkey Breeding Farm, and Bosque del Apache National Wildlife Refuge.

Clarion Books
a Houghton Mifflin Company imprint
52 Vanderbilt Avenue, New York, NY 10017
Text copyright © 1989 by Dorothy Hinshaw Patent
Photographs copyright © 1989 by William Muñoz

For information about permission to reproduce selections from this book, write to Permissions, Houghton Mifflin Company, 2 Park Street, Boston, MA 02108.
Printed in Italy.

Library of Congress Cataloging-in-Publication Data
Patent, Dorothy Hinshaw.
Wild turkey, tame turkey / by Dorothy Hinshaw Patent; photographs by William Muñoz
p. cm.
Includes index.
Summary: Relates the colorful history of the native North American turkey and compares that proud bird with its domesticated cousin.
ISBN 0-89919-704-3
1. Wild turkeys—Juvenile literature. 2. Turkeys—Juvenile literature. [1. Wild turkeys. 2. Turkeys.] I. Muñoz, William, ill. II. Title.
QL696.G254P38 1989   89-613
598′.619—dc19   CIP AC

NI 10 9 8 7 6 5 4 3 2 1

Endpapers: Domesticated turkeys raised on a turkey farm.

To the Musters of Thompson Falls, Montana,
whose efforts to help the wild turkeys through the winter
provide them with a safe refuge.

CONTENTS

Chapter 1

A TRULY AMERICAN BIRD

Turkey—just the word is enough to make some people snicker. To be called a turkey means nothing good. Yet Benjamin Franklin wanted the turkey rather than the bald eagle to be our national bird. What has happened since then to give this impressive native bird such a bad reputation? Domestication, that's what.

The domesticated turkey has been bred to produce a ridiculously huge mass of white meat on its chest and little more. The bird is literally too dumb to come in out of the rain—tame turkeys have been known to die in a downpour. It can't even breed properly without help from its caretakers. But the wild turkey is something else, one of nature's must cunning creatures. A powerful and intelligent native

A wild turkey stalks the woods.

bird with beautiful glossy, brassy feathers—that's the animal Benjamin Franklin had in mind to symbolize the new nation. In comparing the turkey with the bald eagle, Franklin said, "The Turkey is a much more respectable Bird, and withal a true original native of America."

The Wild Turkey

The wild turkey is enough to impress anyone who sees it for the first time. It can be four feet long from beak to tail tip

(Left) The wild turkey has long, slim legs and a long neck.

(Right) The domesticated turkey has thick legs and a shorter neck than its wild cousin.

and can stand four feet tall. The males, also called *toms* or *gobblers*, average over sixteen pounds in weight, with one record breaker bagged in Michigan weighing almost twenty-four pounds. The females, or *hens*, average over nine pounds, with a very large one weighing close to twelve-and-a-half pounds. The wild turkey is slim compared with the overbred, meaty, domesticated bird, and its neck and. legs are longer. Its multihued brown feathers glisten with a metallic sheen in the sunlight.

A gobbler, or male turkey. Notice the dark breast, beard, and the spur on the back of the left leg.

Hens and gobblers look different in several ways other than size. The male turkeys have more bare skin on the head and neck than the females, and adult males have a "beard"—a tuft of stiff, thin feathers on their chests. The beard may be up to eight inches long. Males also sport sharp spurs on the backs of their legs just above the feet.

The tips of the hen turkey's breast feathers are pale, and she has less bare skin on her head and neck than the gobbler.

The spurs can be over two inches long and are used as weapons on the uncommon occasions when gobblers fight each other. The breast feathers of males have black tips, while those of females have buff-colored tips. This gives the breast of the female an overall lighter color, while that of the male appears darker.

Most of the time, turkeys don't look like the typical chubby image drawn every November by school children. Only toms in courtship present that appearance. When they spread a dramatic fan of tail feathers and puff up the feathers on their bodies, they look like fat, round birds rather than sleek, streamlined ones.

A strutting tom, looking like a Thanksgiving turkey should.

The many shades of a turkey's feathers help it melt into the patchy light of the forest floor.

Wild turkeys are very wary—especially mothers with chicks, which are rarely seen by humans. With their sharp eyesight, the birds can spot people and distinguish them at a glance. Then the turkeys disappear into the underbrush, where their camouflage makes them just about invisible.

Turkeys can fly fast for short distances.

Unlike the domesticated turkey, the wild bird is a powerful flyer. When flushed from its hiding place, the wild turkey spreads its five- to six-foot wings and glides away at up to fifty miles per hour. Even on the ground, the bird is speedy and can run as fast as twenty-five miles per hour.

Before White Settlers

The wild turkey once inhabited territory covered by thirty-nine of our present states. Its range extended from just over the northern border into Ontario, Canada, all the way to southern Mexico, and as far west as Wisconsin in the north and Arizona in the south. The Indians in the East hunted turkeys for food. Turkey feathers were made into cloaks to keep people warm during bitter winters. Turkey bones were used to make awls, beads, and spoons. Spurs from toms tipped Indian arrows, while turkey feathers helped the arrows fly true.

In the Southwest, the mysterious Anasazi people domesticated the bird and used its feathers to make blankets and warm leggings. When Europeans arrived in the Americas, they were impressed by this new, large bird. The explorer Castañeda, who traveled with Coronado on his expeditions into the Southwest, marveled at these "cocks with great hanging chins."

The Aztec Indians in Mexico also domesticated the turkey. Spanish explorers reached Mexico in the late 1400s and early 1500s. When they returned to Spain, they took turkeys along with them. These impressive birds became very popular in Spain—large birds with such tasty meat made ideal barnyard fowl. By 1530, domesticated turkeys were also being raised in France, Italy, and England. Later on, American colonists brought this tame version with them when they settled in the new land.

Chapter 2

TURKEYS ALMOST DISAPPEAR

T he coming of the white settlers was a disaster for the turkey as well as for native peoples and other native animals such as the bison. The settlers hunted these bountiful birds and cleared their forest habitats to create farmland. New diseases brought in with domesticated birds also may have hit wild turkeys hard. The effect on turkey numbers was dramatic. By 1861, the wild turkey was practically extinct in Wisconsin. The last wild birds were seen in Massachusetts in 1851, in Ohio in 1878, and in Iowa in 1907. At the lowest point, the wild turkey's range was reduced to one-tenth its original size, and the bird had disappeared completely from almost half the states where it originally lived, as well as from southern Canada.

A small flock of wild turkeys.

Rescuing the Turkey

Around the turn of the century, people realized that something had to be done to reverse the drastic decline in turkey numbers. Laws were put into effect to limit hunting, and preserves were set aside where turkeys were protected. Wild turkeys were so nervous and wary of humans that they couldn't be kept in pens without injuring themselves. For this reason, birds bred on game farms were released into the wild to repopulate where turkeys had once thrived. The game farm birds, however, were domesticated stock or

Turkeys cross the road on the Bosque del Apache

hybrids between domesticated and wild turkeys. Unfortunately, these farm-raised birds consistently died out in the wild. The very traits that allowed them to tolerate life in pens made it impossible for them to survive on their own. They were not alert enough to avoid danger, not ready to take off at the first sign of danger. This kept them from battering themselves against the cages, but it made them easy prey when removed from the protection of humans. The wildness of the wild birds, however, was what made them successful in the woods. They knew how to escape from

National Wildlife Refuge in New Mexico.

danger. When game managers realized this problem, they began releasing wild-caught birds into new areas, and the wild turkey was on the way to recovery.

Wild Turkeys Today

Restocking and careful management of the birds and the land fortunately saved the wild turkey. By 1965, twenty-six states had enough birds to allow hunting, and almost 100,000 birds were bagged. At that time, there were about 750,000 wild turkeys spread out through thirty-five states. Now there are over 1.25 million turkeys living in forty-two states (three more states than before the arrival of the white settlers), and thirty-six of these states permit turkey hunting. Texas alone harbors over .5 million.

There are actually six different types, or subspecies, of wild turkey. All belong to the same species and can interbreed, but they are adapted to life in different habitats. The first scientific description of the turkey was of the domesticated birds brought to Europe during the 1500s from Mexico. These were developed from one subspecies. Another, the Merriam turkey, which is native to the southwestern mountains of Arizona and New Mexico, has been introduced into northern and western states such as Montana, where turkeys didn't live before. Rio Grande turkeys from western Texas have been successfully transplanted to California but not to eastern Texas, where heavier rainfall makes the habitat inappropriate for them.

A Merriam turkey.

Another subspecies is found only in Mexico. The Eastern turkey, which has darker feathers than western types, thrives in the woodlands of the northeastern states. The variety that inhabits Florida is significantly smaller than the Eastern turkey, but looks very similar. The Florida turkey is the smallest subspecies.

THE WILY WILD TURKEY 3

T he wild turkey was able to make such a dramatic comeback because of its great adaptability, its wariness, and its intelligence. It seems that wild turkeys were not afraid of humans when the first colonists arrived. But over time, only the most shy and wary birds survived to reproduce, so that now wild turkeys are rarely observed in areas where they are hunted.

Finding Food

Like most wild animals, turkeys must spend the largest part of their time looking for food and eating. These birds are omnivorous—they eat both animal and plant material. During most of the year, the birds travel in family flocks—a hen

Turkeys hunt for insects and grass seeds.

with her offspring of the year and perhaps a gobbler or two. The older gobblers often stick together in their own small flocks. While turkeys live in open woodlands, they often feed in fields and meadows. They stride through the grass with their heads down, pecking here and there, picking up insects and seeds as they go. The turkeys cluck at one another, which helps maintain a comfortable distance between birds.

Turkeys also feed among the leaf litter on the forest floor for acorns and other tree seeds. The feeding turkey scratches with a set pattern. First it gives a long scratch with its powerful left foot, then two more rapid ones with the right. It finishes off with a long, deep scratch of the left foot. After looking up to check for danger, the bird lowers its head and looks for food among the upturned leaves and soil. When a group of turkeys has fed in an area, it looks as if pigs have been rooting through the ground.

Roosting Time

As twilight begins, the birds head for their nighttime roosts. Turkeys spend the night in the branches of trees, safely protected from predators such as coyotes. Dozens of birds may roost together in the same area. At the first sign of dawn, the birds become restless and soon leave the roost.

A turkey roosting at nightfall.

In the late winter or early spring, those quiet moments of dawn may be broken by the sudden outburst of sound that gives male turkeys their name—the gobble. The gobble is the only strictly seasonal call given by turkeys, and only males make it. The burst of noise begins with startling sharpness, then descends in both tone and loudness as the gobble fades out. A gobbling turkey can be heard a mile away on a still day.

By this time of year, the family flocks have broken up. The hens are attracted for mating by toms gobbling. The male turkeys are stimulated to gobble by almost any unexpected sound—the cawing of a crow or the hoot of an owl, a car door slamming or an airplane overhead. The sound of a female turkey yelping will also bring on gobbling.

Strutting

The gobblers put on a spectacular display for the females during courtship. The bare skin on their naked heads and upper necks becomes bright blue during the breeding season, and a blue blob of skin, called the *snood*, is obvious above the beak. As the bird displays, it can change the color of its skin from whitish blue to brilliant scarlet within moments. The blue color is caused by a pigment, or coloration, in the skin. The rush of red is brought on by an increase in blood circulation to the area. The snood may

Strutting toms.

A tom, with its tail fan gloriously displayed, faces a hen.

appear quite small one moment, then enlarge and droop down over one side of the beak within seconds as more blood flows into it.

The displaying gobbler lifts his head up high as he tucks in his chin. He raises his tail and fans out its beautiful, multicolored feathers. With his body puffed up, he lowers his wings so that their tips touch the ground. The gobbler's appearance is very stiff, and he walks slowly, then takes a few quick steps toward the female while making a soft, hollow *chunk* sound. His wings rustle as they drag along the ground. He rotates his tail fan so that it faces the female during the display and finishes off the whole performance with a gobble.

During all this, the female may act uninterested and peck at the ground. But if she is ready to mate, she will approach the male in a crouched position, and mating will take place.

Strutting toms with reluctant hens.

Chapter

RAISING A FAMILY 4

The turkey hen makes her crude nest in the forest undergrowth near a clearing or meadow. There she lays her spotted, cream-colored eggs one by one. It takes the hen two weeks to produce her clutch of ten to twelve eggs. Hatching comes about four weeks after the last egg is laid. When the turkey chicks are ready to hatch in late May or early June, they peep softly from inside the shells, and their mother answers with a quiet yelping sound. After all the chicks have hatched and dried out their fluffy feathers, the hen walks slowly away from the nest, calling to her babies to follow.

These captive wild turkey chicks are just a few weeks old. When grown up, their feathers will be as big as the one in the foreground, which the hen dropped.

The youngsters, called *poults*, join their mother, and they are on their way to the clearing to feed. Turkey poults grow fast and need plenty of protein, so the weedy open areas full of insects are vital to their survival.

The young birds find their own food, but they stay close to their mother. Until the chicks can fly, the mother roosts on the ground at night, usually near the protective base of a tree. The chicks snuggle under her body and wings, where they are warm and safe.

By the time they are two weeks old, the poults can already fly short distances. Then they are able to roost in the trees like adult turkeys. If danger threatens while the young birds are on the ground, the hen lets out a high, piercing warning call, and the poults flutter up into the protection of nearby branches. The mother flies farther away, which may distract the predator from the chicks. When all seems clear, the chicks cheep for their mother. But she waits to return to them until everything looks completely safe.

Each hen has her own distinctive voice, which her chicks recognize. When the chicks are very young, they never stray far from their mothers. But when they get older and wander, they come back to her when she calls, following the sound of her familiar voice.

The notes of the young birds change as they get older. Their soft *cheep* becomes a louder *kee-kee-kee*. Their voices also get raspier with time, and eventually the male and female birds sound quite different.

By twelve weeks of age, the poults are beginning to look like turkeys and are ready to be released into the wild.

Growing Up

As summer passes, broods join one another to form larger feeding flocks with as many as fifty birds. They eat berries, ripening grass seeds, and mushrooms as well as insects and nuts. If food is scarce, the birds can scratch deeply enough into the forest floor to dig up the bulbs and tubers of woodland plants.

By November, the young turkeys are already quite large. Hen poults weigh six to eight pounds, while young gobblers tip the scales at ten to thirteen pounds. Growth then slows until they reach their final adult size.

During the fall, the turkeys range far and wide in search of food. But as winter approaches, food becomes scarce, and the birds must conserve energy. They break into the smaller family flocks, and their activity lessens. The cold weather and the snow slow them down.

During the winter, the birds cover only about one-tenth of their summer range.

When spring returns, the year-old hens are already able to breed. But the young gobblers require more time. It takes about three years for a tom to grow his long beard and to become large and strong enough to win the right to a sizeable number of females.

A mixed flock of hens and gobblers.

THE TURKEY BUSINESS

Chapter 5

H undreds of years and many generations have passed since the turkey was first domesticated, so it is no wonder that tame turkeys are so different from their wild cousins. Superficially, a bronze-colored domestic turkey looks similar to a wild one. But the skin on its head is fleshier, there's more of it, and it stays red all year-round. Its build is more compact overall. It has shorter, stockier legs, a thicker, shorter neck, and a chubbier body.

While the wild turkey is a powerful short-distance flyer, the domesticated bird can't fly at all when full grown. Its body is too heavy for its wings to lift from the ground. Domesticated turkeys are so heavy that they can't mate nat-

Both bronze-colored and white domesticated turkeys show extensive red skin on their necks.

urally. Sperm is taken from the males and put by specialized workers into the reproductive tracts of the females. This process is called *artificial insemination*.

The most common kind of domesticated turkey is pure white in color. Only the red skin on its head resembles that of wild turkeys. Most large farms raise the white turkeys, although some smaller breeders still use the bronze-colored ones. When a bronze-colored bird is plucked, some pigment from the feathers may leak under the skin. This gives the skin dark spots. Since white feathers have no pigment, the plucked white bird has clear, even-colored skin that looks much more appealing to the buyer.

The biggest differences between wild and domesticated turkeys lie inside the birds, in their personality and character. Domesticated turkeys may set up a loud chorus of complaint when a stranger enters their barn, but they approach familiar humans willingly. Wild turkeys, on the other hand, avoid humans. The domestic birds have also lost the wily intelligence and survival instincts of their free-living cousins, but their human caretakers see to it that they are well fed and protected.

While the heavy domesticated turkeys can't really fly, they can flutter up to the roof with effort before they are fully grown.

These hens have no role in life other than laying eggs that will produce turkeys for eating.

Growing Meat

Raising turkeys for meat has become a science. Unfortunately for the breeding business, successful egg laying and maximum meat production conflict with one another. The breast meat is the most desirable part of the turkey, so breeders want to raise birds that provide the most white meat possible. Growers also want their birds to gain weight quickly and to convert feed efficiently into meat. These are not serious problems for the male birds. But the females need plenty of energy to nourish the large eggs. And they need to put energy into egg production rather than into adding and maintaining muscle.

Breeders have solved this problem in a fascinating way. Certain growers specialize in raising male and female turkeys for breeding instead of raising birds for eating. These growers produce two different lines of turkeys. Although each line has male and female birds, one line is called the *male line*, and the other is called the *female line*. Male and female birds in the male line become very large. They grow fast and turn feed into meat very efficiently. The female-line birds are smaller. They don't need to use as much energy to fuel a big body, so they can lay more eggs than male-line hens.

Of course, each strain produces both male and female birds. But when it comes time to get the eggs that will be hatched into birds for market, sperm from the male strain is used to fertilize female birds from the female strain. The eggs these birds produce hatch into chicks that will end up on Thanksgiving tables.

Turkey Specialists

The turkey-growing business has become very specialized, with only four companies in the world producing all the eggs used to get breeding stock. These large companies send male- and female-line eggs to hatcheries. Turkey farmers then get poults from the hatchery and raise the turkeys for breeding. The hens are ready to breed at about thirty weeks of age. They are housed together in a large building that is kept lit from fourteen to fifteen hours a day. This prolonged light stimulates the hens to lay eggs.

Once a week the hens are artificially inseminated with sperm from male-line birds. Each hen starts out laying about five eggs a week. After twenty-five weeks, egg production slows down. Many growers send the hens to be slaughtered at this age. But others give them a rest for three months and then have them lay for another twenty-five-week cycle before having them slaughtered. The meat from spent hens is tough, so it is usually used in making soup.

(Right) A hen on a nest. This fortunate bird lives on a small farm and is being allowed to incubate her own eggs.

(Below) Egg-laying hens. These birds have more room than turkeys being raised for meat. If the hens are too crowded, they won't lay eggs.

FROM HATCHERY TO TABLE 6

T he eggs that will hatch into turkeys for the table are washed, dried, and packed into boxes. Then they are shipped to the hatchery.

At the Hatchery

A modern turkey hatchery has huge incubators that hold thousands of eggs each. Thermostats keep the temperature between 99.5° and 99.7° F and the humidity at 86 percent. After about two weeks of incubation, the growing chicks inside the eggs produce enough heat to keep the incubators warm. Sometimes a cooling fan must be used to keep the temperature from getting too hot.

Trays of turkey eggs in an incubator. Normally, the heavy, insulated door is closed so that the temperature can be carefully regulated.

48

Inside the incubator, the trays of eggs are tipped 45° in each direction once an hour. This imitates the natural action of the hen, who turns her eggs in the nest. If the eggs aren't turned, the embryos stick to the shells, and the chicks can't hatch normally.

As with wild turkeys, the eggs hatch after twenty-eight days. When the eggs are ready to hatch, they are moved into hatchers, where the temperature is kept at 98° F and the humidity at 87 percent. The very first step in hatching is a tiny hole the chick makes in the shell with the special egg tooth that grows on top of its beak. The cramped chick turns its body as it pecks its way through the tough membrane that lines the inside of the shell. Hatching is a difficult task—it takes two to three days from the first crack until the chick actually climbs out of the shell.

(Left) The eggs begin to hatch. Notice the hole pecked by the chick in the egg in the center of the picture.

(Right) The wet chick struggles to free itself from its shell.

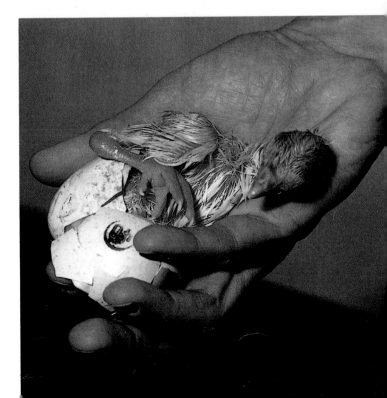

A drawerful of newly hatched chicks in an opened hatcher.

A few hours after the chicks hatch and their feathers dry out, they are readied for market. Expert workers examine them to separate the males from the females. The chicks are given shots containing B vitamins and antibiotics. Because the birds will be raised in close quarters, they must be protected from hurting one another, so the sharp tips of their beaks are snipped off, and their claws are clipped. The snoods of male chicks are removed so others can't pull on them. This is all done very quickly and efficiently. The chicks are then packed in boxes and shipped to the farms where they will be raised for the table.

...ted chicks under the warm light of an incubator

Raising Turkeys

Once they reach the grower, the chicks are crowded into large buildings with low roofs. A typical turkey barn is forty by five hundred feet and holds seven thousand toms or ten thousand hens. During the summer months, some breeders keep the birds outside. They are fed specially formulated

A houseful of young turkeys.

food to help them gain weight as fast as possible. These birds are bred to be slaughtered when only a few months old, so they must grow very quickly.

The birds gain weight so fast that hens are ready for slaughter in only sixteen weeks. By then, a hen will have reached the size of a twelve pound, ready-to-cook turkey. The toms, which require more protein to reach full size, are ready in nineteen weeks. They are sold at a ready-to-cook weight of eighteen to twenty pounds. Sometimes they are allowed to get bigger. A domesticated tom can go from one-and-one-third ounces at hatching in the spring to almost thirty-five pounds in six months, by Thanksgiving. Large size is one thing turkey breeders have worked for. While the heaviest wild turkey on record weighed less than twenty-four pounds, the record domesticated bird totaled seventy-five pounds.

Turkey at the Supermarket

The biggest sales of turkeys used to be for Thanksgiving and Christmas dinners. Ninety-five percent of all turkeys were once sold during the last two months of the year. But today, 60 percent of the turkeys grown are eaten during other times of the year. Turkey ham, turkey bologna, and other processed meat are found in every supermarket, and boneless breast and ground turkey are also sold. Turkey is a tasty, low-fat food that most people like. It is also relatively inexpensive.

The modern methods of breeding and raising turkeys have made this healthful, low-cost food available to everyone year-round. But in order to make this possible, turkeys are raised in confined conditions. The farmers take good care of them, for unhealthy birds won't grow quickly and sell well. However, some people are concerned about the welfare of turkeys and other farm animals raised in crowded circumstances. Do the birds suffer, or doesn't it bother them to live in this way? These are questions that are difficult for us to answer. But as farming becomes more and more of a science, they are important issues to think about.

INDEX

Page numbers in *italics* refer to captions.